PRE-APPRENTICESHIP
MATHS & LITERACY FOR
ELECTRICAL (PART II)

Graduated exercises and practice exam

Andrew Spencer

A+ National Pre-apprenticeship Maths & Literacy for Electrical (Part II)
1st Edition
Andrew Spencer

Publishing editors: Sarah Broomhall and Jennifer Down
Project editor: Aynslie Harper
Editor: Anna Pang
Text designer: Miranda Costa
Cover designer: Aisling Gallagher
Cover image: Shutterstock.com/Lighthunter
Production controller: Emily Moore
Typeset by: Q2A Media
Reprint: Katie McCappin

Any URLs contained in this publication were checked for currency during the production process. Note, however, that the publisher cannot vouch for the ongoing currency of URLs.

For product information and technology assistance,
in Australia call **1300 790 853**;
in New Zealand call **0800 449 725**

For permission to use material from this text or product, please email **aust.permissions@cengage.com**

ISBN 978 0 17 047453 5

Cengage Learning Australia
Level 7, 80 Dorcas Street
South Melbourne, Victoria Australia 3205

Cengage Learning New Zealand
Unit 4B Rosedale Office Park
331 Rosedale Road, Albany, North Shore 0632, NZ

For learning solutions, visit **cengage.com.au**

Printed in Australia by Ligare Pty Limited.
1 2 3 4 5 6 7 26 25 24 23 22

A+ National
PRE-APPRENTICESHIP
Maths & Literacy for Electrical (Part II)

Contents

9780170474535

Introduction

It has always been important to understand, from a teacher's perspective, the nature of the mathematical skills students need for their future, rather than teaching them textbook mathematics. This has been a guiding principle behind the development of the content in this workbook. To teach maths that is *relevant* to students seeking apprenticeships is the best that we can do, to give students an education in the field that they would like to work in.

The content in this resource is aimed at the level that is needed for a student to have the best possibility of improving their maths and literacy skills specifically for trades. Students can use this workbook to prepare for an apprenticeship entry assessment, or even to assist with basic numeracy and literacy at the VET/TAFE level. Coupled with the activities on the NelsonNet website, https://www.nelsonnet.com.au/free-resources, these resources have the potential to improve the students' understanding of basic mathematical concepts that can be applied to trades. These resources have been trialled, and they work.

Commonly used trade terms are introduced so that students have a basic understanding of terminology that they will encounter in the workplace environment. Students who can complete this workbook and reach an 80 per cent or higher outcome in all topics will have achieved the goal of this resource. These students will go on to complete work experience, do a VET accredited course, or be able to gain entry into VET/TAFE or an apprenticeship in the trade of their choice.

The content in this workbook is the first step towards bridging the gap between what has been learnt in previous years, and what needs to be remembered and re-learnt for use in trades. Students will significantly benefit from the consolidation of the basic maths and literacy concepts.

Every school has students who want to work with their hands, and not all students want to go to university. The best students want to learn what they don't know, and if students want to learn, then this book has the potential to give them a good start in life.

This resource has been specifically tailored to prepare students for sitting apprenticeship or VET/TAFE admission tests, and for giving students the basic skills they will need for a career in trade. In many ways, it is a win–win situation, with students enjoying and studying relevant maths for work, and for Trades and Registered Training Officers (RTOs) receiving students who have improved basic maths and literacy skills.

All that is needed from students is patience, hard work, a positive attitude, a belief in themselves that they can do it and a desire to achieve.

About the author

Andrew Spencer graduated from SACAE Underdale in 1988, with a Bachelor of Education. In 1989, he went on to attend West Virginia University, where he completed a Master of Science (specialising in teacher education), while lecturing part time.

In 1993, Andrew moved to NSW and began teaching at Sydney Boys' High, where he taught in a range of subject areas including Mathematics, English, Science, Classics, Physical Education and Technical Studies. His sense of practical mathematics continued to develop with the range of subject areas he taught.

Andrew moved back to South Australia in 1997 with a diverse knowledge base and an understanding of the importance of using mathematics in different practical subject areas. He began teaching with the De La Salle Brothers in 1997 in South Australia, where he continues to work and teach today. Andrew has worked in collaboration with the SACE Board to help develop resources for Mathematics with a practical focus.

In 2011, Andrew was awarded the John Gaffney Mathematics Education Trust Award for valuable contributions to the teaching of Mathematics in South Australia. He received a Recognition of Excellence for outstanding contributions to the teaching profession by CEASA in 2011 and 2012 and, in 2014, he was one of 12 teachers from across Australia to work in collaboration with the Chief Scientist of Australia to develop a better understanding of the role of mathematics in industry. As part of this role, he undertook research in this area, spent time working with the industry, and then fed the results back to the Chief Scientist.

Andrew continues to develop the pre-apprenticeship and vocational titles, based on mathematics and literacy, to assist and support the learning of students who want to follow a vocational career path. The titles have also been adapted in the UK and Asia, as the importance of this type of functional maths continues to grow. All schools have students who will follow a vocational pathway and it continues to be a strong focus of Andrew's to support the learning needs of these students.

Author acknowledgements

For Paula, Zach, Katelyn, Mum and Dad.

To the De La Salle Brothers for their selfless work with all students.

To Dr Pauline Carter for her unwavering support of all Mathematics teachers.

To all students who value learning, who are willing to work hard and who have character … and are characters!

LITERACY

Unit 1: Spelling

Short-answer questions

Specific instructions to students

- This is an exercise to help you to identify and correct spelling errors.
- Read the activity below and then answer accordingly.

Read the following passage, and identify and correct the spelling errors.

Luke, the aprentice electrisian, wanted to research the use of electricity in a home, particularly about how it is set up. He found that with electricity in the home, the powar flows through the meter box, which measures the units of electrical energy that are used. This is mesured in kilowats per hour (kW/h). The electricity then passes through a main switch that has the abillity to cut off the electricity alltogether should repairs and/or certan changes need to be made to the wirring. The electricity is then carried to a fuse board and/or circuit breaker where branch circuits then transfur the electricity throughout the house.

Luke knew that electricity runs in a circut and that all electricel apliances must have at least two wires. These include the active wire (used to cary electricity from the genarator), and the nutral wire (which acts to return the electricity to the generator). Zach, who is also an apprentice electrician, told Luke that in the fuse bord there is a fuse/circuit breaker that has been instaled for each circuit of the house. These circuits include the lights, any power outlet, the hot water system and any appliance that uses electricity. Luke told Zach that the role of the fuses or circuit braker is to protact the wiring in any home.

Incorrect words:

_____

_____

Correct words:

_____

_____

Unit 2: Alphabetising

Short-answer questions

Specific instructions to students

- In this unit, you will be able to practise your alphabetising skills.
- Read the activity below and then answer accordingly.

Put the following words into alphabetical order.

Lineman's pliers	Stud detector
Diagonal cutters	Wire strippers
Insulated screwdrivers	Long nose pliers
Heavy-duty cable cutters	Butane blow torch
Crimpers	Hole saw kit
Tool bag and belt	Voltage detector
Hex key set	Hi-vis safety vest

Answer:

_____

_____

_____

_____

_____

_____

_____

_____

_____

_____

_____

_____

_____

Unit 3: Comprehension

Specific instructions to students

- This is an exercise to help you understand what you read.
- Read the following activity and then answer the questions that follow.

Read the following passage and answer the questions using full sentences.

Two electrical apprentices, Andrew and Grace, are talking with their training instructor Mark about safety and home circuits. Grace asks Mark, 'What's so important about safety switches or residual current devices (RCDs)?' Mark answers, 'They are important devices for guarding us against electric shock and they are kept in the fuse box next to a circuit breaker or the fuses'. Andrew then asks, 'Yeah, but what do they *actually* do?' 'They are safety devices that can detect leaks from currents from faulty switches, wiring or electrical appliances. If the safety switch detects any problems that could put you in danger, it'll turn the power off in less than a second! Even within 0.03 of a second!', answers Mark. 'Oh, that makes sense', replies Grace. 'I've read that every safety switch has a "test" button, to make sure that they're working', adds Andrew.

'What about earth wires?' asks Grace. 'Earth wires are really important because they are specifically designed to protect us from electric shock', states Mark. 'Where are they attached?' asks Andrew. 'They are attached to any power points that are also joined to a main earth wire. The earth wire is then attached to a metal pipe or distinctive metal stake that has been positioned in the ground. The electricity is therefore given a preferred conductive path to the earth rather than entering a person', said Mark.

'Have you read up on surge diverters at all?' asks Mark. Grace exclaims, 'I have! Surge diverters protect your electrical appliances from surges that may be caused by lightning strikes or other voltage surges. A bad thing is that they don't protect people from electric shock'. Mark then asks his students, 'Does the surge diverter arrest any voltage spikes in the wiring in the unit?' 'Yes, it does', answers Grace. 'That will make sure that any voltage spike or surge will not transfer into your appliance and damage them', adds Mark.

QUESTION 1

Why are safety switches or residual current devices (RCDs) important as safety devices?

Answer:

_____

_____

QUESTION 2

How do safety switches or RCDs work to keep people safe in their homes?

Answer:

_____

_____

QUESTION 3

What is the role of earth wires and where would you find them?

Answer:

_____

_____

_____

QUESTION 4

Why are earth wires attached to a metal pipe or metal stake in the ground?

Answer:

_____

_____

QUESTION 5

What is the role of surge diverters and what is one of their limitations?

Answer:

_____

_____

_____

9780170474535

MATHEMATICS

Unit 4: Estimation

Section A: Addition and subtraction

Short-answer questions

Specific instructions to students

- This section will help you to improve your estimation skills.
- Read the following questions and answer all of them in the spaces provided.
- You may *not* use a calculator.
- You need to show all working.

Estimate the following by rounding each value to the nearest whole number, ten or hundred, as appropriate.

QUESTION 1

$0.9\,W + 1.2\,W$

Answer:

QUESTION 2

$4.8\,\Omega + 9.7\,\Omega$

Answer:

QUESTION 3

$24.4\,V - 12.2\,V$

Answer:

QUESTION 4

$68.9\,W - 31.1\,W$

Answer:

QUESTION 5

$1.8\,\Omega \times 3.1\,\Omega$

Answer:

QUESTION 6

$11.2\,V \times 39.8\,V$

Answer:

QUESTION 7

$0.8\,W \div 0.9\,W$

Answer:

QUESTION 8

$19.2\,\Omega \div 2.3\,\Omega$

Answer:

Section B: Worded estimation problems

QUESTION 1

A stereo uses 200 W per hour at a party and is on for seven hours. How many watts have been used?

Answer:

_____

QUESTION 2

A vacuum cleaner uses 750 W per hour and is used for three hours. How many watts have been used?

Answer:

_____

QUESTION 3

A strip heater uses 2000 W per hour in a shed while the footy is on and is left on for 6 hours and 45 minutes. Estimate how many watts are used for this time.

Answer:

_____

QUESTION 4

An air conditioner uses 3250 W per hour and is used for 11.2 hours on a hot day.

a   Estimate the number of watts used.

Answer:

_____

The temperature climbs again later in the week and the air conditioner is left running for a total of 78 hours.

b   Estimate the number of watts used during the week.

Answer:

_____

QUESTION 5

A laptop uses 180 W while it is running and is left on for 7 hours and 50 minutes during the day. Estimate the number of watts used.

Answer:

_____

Section C: Estimation using a wattage table

Short-answer questions

Specific instructions to students

- This section will help you to improve your estimation skills using a wattage table.
- Read the following questions and answer all of them in the spaces provided.
- You may *not* use a calculator.
- You need to show all working.

Use the information in the table to estimate the watts used in the questions below.

Appliance	Est. watts per hour	Appliance	Est. watts per hour
DVD player	35	Clock radio	50
Christmas lights (string of 50)	25	Blender	300
Table fan	230	Washing machine	920
Hotplate	1200	Xbox	100
Laptop computer	60	Freezer	500−800

QUESTION 1

How many watts are used by a clock radio that is left on for 24 hours (one day)?

Answer:

QUESTION 2

A blender is used for 30 minutes. How many watts are used?

Answer:

QUESTION 3

A table fan is left on for 5 hours and 20 minutes. Estimate how many watts are used.

Answer:

QUESTION 4

A washing machine takes 45 minutes to complete a wash cycle. Estimate the number of watts used.

Answer:

QUESTION 5

An Xbox is used for six and three quarter hours. Estimate the number of watts used.

Answer:

QUESTION 6

A DVD player plays a movie that goes for 2 hours and 50 minutes. Estimate the watts used.

Answer:

QUESTION 7

A string of 50 Christmas lights is used for 28 days during December. It is switched on at 8 p.m. and left on until 7.30 a.m. each day. Estimate how many watts are used during December.

QUESTION 8

Three hotplates on a stovetop are used continuously for six hours and ten minutes to cook food for a wedding reception. Estimate the total number of watts used.

Answer:

_____

_____

_____

QUESTION 9

A freezer draws 650 W per hour and is left on 24/7 for a year. Estimate the total number of watts used.

Answer:

_____

_____

_____

_____

QUESTION 10

A laptop is used for 15 minutes to check emails. Estimate the total number of watts used.

Answer:

_____

9780170474535

Unit 5: An Introduction to Algebra

Section A: Addition

Use the following example to answer the questions.

> **EXAMPLE**
>
> Simplify the expression $6a + 2a$.
>
> $6a + 2a = 8a$

Simplify the following expressions.

QUESTION 1

$2a + 7a$

Answer:

_____

QUESTION 2

$3b + 5b$

Answer:

_____

QUESTION 3

$6c + 8c$

Answer:

_____

QUESTION 4

$9n + 13n$

Answer:

_____

QUESTION 5

$11v + 19v$

Answer:

_____

Section B: Subtraction

Use the following example to answer the questions.

> **EXAMPLE**
>
> Simplify the expression $5h - 2h$.
>
> $5h - 2h = 3h$

Simplify the following expressions.

QUESTION 1

$4d - 1d$

Answer:

_____

QUESTION 2

$7t - 4t$

Answer:

_____

QUESTION 3

$11h - 7h$

Answer:

_____

QUESTION 4

$15j - 8j$

Answer:

_____

QUESTION 5

$22a - 13a$

Answer:

_____

Section C: Multiplication

Short-answer questions

Specific instructions to students

- This section will help you to improve your multiplication skills when working with algebra.
- Read the following questions below and answer all of them in the spaces provided.
- You may *not* use a calculator.
- You will need to show all working.

Use the following example to answer the questions.

EXAMPLE

Simplify the expression $3f \times 2g$.

$3f \times 2g = 6fg$

Simplify the following expressions.

QUESTION 1

$2a \times 7x$

Answer:

_____

QUESTION 2

$4m \times 8v$

Answer:

_____

QUESTION 3

$5j \times 9h$

Answer:

_____

QUESTION 4

$7g \times 6r$

Answer:

_____

QUESTION 5

$8d \times 7p$

Answer:

_____

QUESTION 6

$16r \times 13b$

Answer:

_____

9780170474535

Section D: Division

Specific instructions to students

- This section will help you to improve your division skills when working with algebra.
- Read the following questions below and answer all of them in the spaces provided.
- You may *not* use a calculator.
- You will need to show all working.

Use the following example to answer the questions.

EXAMPLE

Simplify the expression $\dfrac{4r}{2}$.

$$\dfrac{4r}{2} = 2r$$

Simplify the following expressions.

QUESTION 1

$\dfrac{6t}{2}$

Answer:

QUESTION 2

$\dfrac{9}{3e}$

Answer:

QUESTION 3

$\dfrac{14p}{2p}$

Answer:

QUESTION 4

$\dfrac{21w}{7w}$

Answer:

QUESTION 5

$\dfrac{36y}{6y}$

Answer:

QUESTION 6

$\dfrac{96}{8a}$

Answer:

QUESTION 7

$\dfrac{144}{12m}$

Answer:

QUESTION 8

$\dfrac{110j}{10}$

Answer:

Unit 6: Collecting Like Terms

Section A: Addition and subtraction

Short-answer questions

Specific instructions to students

- This section will help you to improve your addition and subtraction skills when collecting like terms.
- Read the following questions and answer all of them in the spaces provided.
- You may *not* use a calculator.
- You need to show all working.

Use the following examples to answer the questions.

EXAMPLE

$4r - 3c + 2r = 4r + 2r - 3c$

$\qquad\qquad = 6r - 3c$

EXAMPLE

$6e + 4f - 3e = 6e - 3e + 4f$

$\qquad\qquad = 3e + 4f$

Simplify the following expressions.

QUESTION 1

$2a - 4t + 3a$

Answer:

_____

QUESTION 2

$3c + 7c - 6r$

Answer:

_____

QUESTION 3

$4f - 9i + 6f$

Answer:

_____

QUESTION 4

$5q + 4k - 2k$

Answer:

_____

QUESTION 5

$8f - 2f + 7y$

Answer:

_____

QUESTION 6

$11p - 12p - 5e$

Answer:

_____

QUESTION 7

$34j - 16e + 27j$

Answer:

_____

QUESTION 8

$53b + 39b - 18i$

Answer:

_____

9780170474535

Section B: Multiplication and division

Short-answer questions

Specific instructions to students

- This section will help you to improve your multiplication and division skills when collecting like terms.
- Read the following questions below and answer all of them in the spaces provided.
- You may *not* use a calculator.
- You will need to show all working.

Use the following example to answer questions 1 to 5.

EXAMPLE

Simplify the expression $8j \times 4$

$8j \times 4 = 32j$

Simplify the following expressions.

QUESTION 1

$3y \times 9$

Answer:

QUESTION 2

$7k \times 8$

Answer:

QUESTION 3

$12p \times 11$

Answer:

QUESTION 4

$10h \times 8$

Answer:

QUESTION 5

$24 \times 3m$

Answer:

Use the following example to answer questions 6 to 10.

EXAMPLE

$\dfrac{3d}{2} + \dfrac{2d}{3} = \dfrac{9d}{6} + \dfrac{4d}{6}$ The lowest common denominator is 6

$\qquad = \dfrac{13d}{6}$

QUESTION 6

$\dfrac{3c}{3} + \dfrac{4c}{4} = c + c$

Answer:

QUESTION 7

$\dfrac{5g}{5} - \dfrac{2g}{6} = \dfrac{30g}{30} - \dfrac{10g}{30}$

Answer:

QUESTION 8

$\dfrac{6y}{3} + \dfrac{8y}{9} = \dfrac{18y}{9} + \dfrac{8y}{9}$

Answer:

QUESTION 9

$\dfrac{12n}{8} - \dfrac{5n}{3} = \dfrac{36n}{24} - \dfrac{40n}{24}$

Answer:

QUESTION 10

$\dfrac{11p}{10} + \dfrac{7p}{2} = \dfrac{11p}{10} + \dfrac{35p}{10}$

Answer:

Unit 7: Expanding Brackets and Collecting Like Terms

Section A: Expanding a single pair of brackets

Use the following example to answer questions 1 to 6.

EXAMPLE

Simplify the expression $3(v - 2)$

$3(v - 2) = 3v - 6$

Simplify the following expressions.

QUESTION 1

$2(x - h)$

Answer:

QUESTION 2

$5(f + b)$

Answer:

QUESTION 3

$7(m - y)$

Answer:

QUESTION 4

$9(2c + 9)$

Answer:

QUESTION 5

$12(5e - b)$

Answer:

QUESTION 6

$14(d + 4)$

Answer:

Use the following example to answer questions 7 to 12.

EXAMPLE

$4(2n + 2) + 2n = 8n + 8 + 2n$

$$= 10n + 8$$

QUESTION 7

$3(6f - 8) + 4f$

$= 18f - 24 + 4f$

Answer:

QUESTION 8

$5(7t + 4) - 12t$

$= 35t + 20 - 12t$

Answer:

QUESTION 9

$6(9k - 9) + 15k$

$= 54k - 54 + 15k$

Answer:

QUESTION 10

$9(10g + 12) - 18g$

$= 90g + 108 - 18g$

Answer:

QUESTION 11

$11(11n - 11) + 22n$

$= 121n - 121 + 22n$

Answer:

QUESTION 12

$13(8a + 12) - 45a$

$= 104a + 156 - 45a$

Answer:

Section B: Expanding and simplifying brackets

Short-answer questions

Specific instructions to students

- This section will help you to improve your ability to expand and simplify brackets, and collect like terms.
- Read the following questions below and answer all of them in the spaces provided.
- You may *not* use a calculator.
- You will need to show all working.

Use the following example to answer questions 1 to 5.

EXAMPLE

$2(y + 4) + 3(y + 3) = 2y + 8 + 3y + 9$

$= 5y + 17$

Simplify the following expressions.

QUESTION 1

$2(k + 3) + 3(k + 8)$

$= 2k + 6 + 3k + 24$

Answer:

QUESTION 2

$4(g - 3) + 5(g + 7)$

$= 4g - 12 + 5g + 35$

Answer:

QUESTION 3

$5(z + 6) + 8(z + 5)$

$= 5z + 30 + 8z + 40$

Answer:

QUESTION 4

$8(h - 4) + 9(h + 4)$

$= 8h - 32 + 9h + 36$

Answer:

QUESTION 5

$9(p + 8) + 7(p + 10)$

$= 9p + 72 + 7p + 70$

Answer:

Use the following example to answer questions 6 to 10.

$$4(f - 2) - 3(f - 2) = 4f - 8 - 3f + 6$$
$$= f - 2$$

QUESTION 6
$3(f - 7) - 3(f - 5)$

$= 3f - 21 - 3f + 15$

Answer:

_____

QUESTION 7
$4(a + 8) - 5(a + 9)$

$= 4a + 32 - 5a - 45$

Answer:

_____

QUESTION 8
$6(t - 9) - 6(t - 7)$

$= 6t - 54 - 6t + 42$

Answer:

_____

QUESTION 9
$8(j + 11) - 8(j + 12)$

$= 8j + 88 - 8j - 96$

Answer:

_____

QUESTION 10
$12(n - 11) - 13(n - 12)$

$= 12n - 132 - 13n + 156$

Answer:

_____

Use the following example to answer questions 11 to 15.

$$p(2y + 4f) + 3p(y + 3f) = 2py + 4pf + 3py + 9pf$$
$$= 5py + 13pf$$

QUESTION 11
$r(3k + 2h) + 2r(k - 2h)$

$= 3rk + 2rh + 2rk - 4rh$

Answer:

_____

QUESTION 12
$n(4d - 3m) - 3n(d + m)$

$= 4nd - 3nm - 3nd - 3nm$

Answer:

_____

QUESTION 13
$a(7b + 5j) + 6a(2b - 8j)$

$= 7ab + 5aj + 12ab - 48aj$

Answer:

_____

QUESTION 14
$v(9c - 6i) - 7v(3c + 8i)$

$= 9vc - 6vi - 21vc - 56vi$

Answer:

_____

QUESTION 15
$y(12s + 7d) + 6y(5s - 5d)$

$12ys + 7yd + 30ys - 30yd$

Answer:

_____

Use the following example to answer questions 16 to 20.

$$\frac{2f}{3} + \frac{f+3}{2} = \frac{4f}{6} + \frac{3(f+3)}{6}$$

The lowest common denominator is 6

$$= \frac{4f}{6} + \frac{3f+9}{6}$$

$$= \frac{7f+9}{6}$$

QUESTION 16

$$\frac{3v}{2} + \frac{5v+5}{4} = \frac{6v}{4} + \frac{5v+5}{4}$$

Answer:

_____

QUESTION 17

$$\frac{6g}{3} - \frac{8g-3}{5} = \frac{30g}{15} - \frac{24g-9}{15}$$

Answer:

_____

QUESTION 18

$$\frac{7j}{6} + \frac{9j+6}{2} = \frac{7j}{6} + \frac{3(9j+6)}{6}$$

$$= \frac{7j}{6} + \frac{27j+18}{6}$$

Answer:

_____

QUESTION 19

$$\frac{10t}{5} - \frac{3t+8}{7} = \frac{7(10t)}{35} - \frac{5(3t+8)}{35}$$

$$= \frac{70t}{35} - \frac{15t+40}{35}$$

Answer:

_____

QUESTION 20

$$\frac{12m}{8} + \frac{6m-2}{9} = \frac{9(12m)}{72} + \frac{8(6m-2)}{72}$$

$$= \frac{108m}{72} + \frac{48m-16}{72}$$

Answer:

_____

Unit 8: Exponents (Powers)

Short-answer questions

Specific instructions to students

- This section will help you to improve your ability to work with exponents.
- Read the following questions and answer all of them in the spaces provided.
- You may *not* use a calculator.
- You need to show all working.

Given the term $2y^3$,
- the coefficient is 2
- the base is y
- the exponent or power is 3.

When an equation is to be simplified, like terms can be collected together.

Use the following example to answer questions 1 to 5.

EXAMPLE

$3m^2 + 2m^2 = 5m^2$

Simplify the following expressions.

QUESTION 1
$4p^2 + 6p^2$

Answer:

QUESTION 2
$6c^3 + 7c^3$

Answer:

QUESTION 3
$8a^2 + 15a^2$

Answer:

QUESTION 4
$22w^3 - 13w^3$

Answer:

QUESTION 5
$31s^2 - 18s^2$

Answer:

Use the following example to answer questions 6 to 9.

EXAMPLE

$$4a^2 + 3a - 2a^2 + 7a - 4 = 4a^2 - 2a^2 + 3a + 7a - 4$$
$$= 2a^2 + 10a - 4$$

QUESTION 6
$5b^2 + 6b - 2b^2 - 2b + 9$

Answer:

QUESTION 7
$8m^3 - 9n + 4m^3 - 3n - 2$

Answer:

QUESTION 8
$15k^2 + 13z^3 - 7k^2 + 8z^3 + k + 16$

Answer:

QUESTION 9
$3r^2 + 22s^3 + 5r^2 - 3s^3 + s - 7$

Answer:

9780170474535

Use the following example to answer questions 10 to 15.

$$\frac{4m^3 + 3}{5} + \frac{2m^3 - 1}{3}$$ The lowest common denominator is 15

$$= \frac{3(4m^3 + 3)}{15} + \frac{5(2m^3 - 1)}{15}$$

$$= \frac{12m^3 + 9}{15} + \frac{10m^3 - 5}{15}$$

$$= \frac{12m^3 + 10m^3 + 9 - 5}{15}$$

$$= \frac{22m^3 + 4}{15}$$

QUESTION 10

$$\frac{5g^3 + 4}{2} + \frac{2g^3 - 6}{3}$$

$$= \frac{3(5g^3 + 4)}{6} + \frac{2(2g^3 - 6)}{6}$$

$$= \frac{15g^3 + 12 + 4g^3 - 12}{6}$$

Answer:

QUESTION 11

$$\frac{7j^2 + 4}{3} + \frac{2j^2 - 3}{2}$$

$$= \frac{2(7j^2 + 4)}{6} + \frac{3(2j^2 - 3)}{6}$$

$$= \frac{14j^2 + 8}{6} + \frac{6j^2 - 9}{6}$$

Answer:

QUESTION 12

$$\frac{a^3 + 4}{3} - \frac{7a^3 + 1}{4}$$

$$= \frac{4(a^3 + 4)}{12} - \frac{3(7a^3 + 1)}{12}$$

$$= \frac{4a^3 + 16}{12} - \frac{21a^3 + 3}{12}$$

Answer:

QUESTION 13

$$\frac{8n^3 + 2r - 2}{5} + \frac{2n^3 - 3r + 3}{4}$$

$$= \frac{4(8n^3 + 2r - 2)}{20} + \frac{5(2n^3 - 3r + 3)}{20}$$

$$= \frac{32n^3 + 8r - 8 + 10n^3 - 15r + 15}{20}$$

Answer:

_____

QUESTION 14

$$\frac{3b^3 + 4c - 3}{2} - \frac{b^3 - 5c + 9}{5}$$

$$= \frac{5(3b^3 + 4c - 3)}{10} - \frac{2(b^3 - 5c + 9)}{10}$$

$$= \frac{15b^3 + 20c - 15}{10} - \frac{2b^3 - 10c + 18}{10}$$

Answer:

_____

QUESTION 15

$$\frac{7x^3 - 5x + 1}{3} + \frac{3x^3 - x - 2}{5}$$

$$= \frac{5(7x^3 - 5x + 1)}{15} + \frac{3(3x^3 - x - 2)}{15}$$

$$= \frac{35x^3 - 25x + 5}{15} + \frac{9x^3 - 3x - 6}{15}$$

Answer:

_____

Unit 9: Solving Equations by Substitution

Short-answer questions

Specific instructions to students

- This section will help you to improve your ability to solve equations by substitution.
- Read the following questions and answer all of them in the spaces provided.
- You may *not* use a calculator.
- You need to show all working.

Use the following example to solve questions 1 to 5.

EXAMPLE

Solve $3 + g$, when $g = 2$

$3 + g = 3 + 2$

$\qquad = 5$

QUESTION 1

Solve $5 + t$, when $t = 7$

Answer:

_____

QUESTION 2

Solve $k - 6$, when $k = 11$

Answer:

_____

QUESTION 3

Solve $27 + y$, when $y = 17$

Answer:

_____

QUESTION 4

Solve $p - 13$, when $p = 13$

Answer:

_____

QUESTION 5

Solve $103 + h$, when $h = 28$

Answer:

_____

Substitute the values $y = 3$ and $k = 8$ into questions 6 to 10 and solve the equations.

QUESTION 6

$3y - k$

Answer:

_____

QUESTION 7

$8k + 5y$

Answer:

_____

QUESTION 8

$\dfrac{3k}{3}$

Answer:

_____

QUESTION 9

$y(4k - 6)$

Answer:

_____

QUESTION 10

$\dfrac{2y + 2k}{y + k}$

Answer:

_____

9780170474535

Unit 10: Solving Electrical Equations by Substitution

Section A: Calculating the number of watts in a circuit

Use the following formula to complete the exercises.

> ### Watts in a circuit
>
> When calculating the number of watts that are in a circuit, the formula that can be used is:
>
> $W = VA$
>
> where
>
> W = power or watts in circuit   (unit is watts, W)
> V = voltage in power source   (unit is volts, V)
> A = amps in power source   (unit is amps, A)

For each question below, calculate the number of watts in a circuit that has the values given, using $W = VA$.

QUESTION 1
When $V = 12$ and $A = 4$.

Answer:

_____

QUESTION 2
When $V = 15$ and $A = 3$.

Answer:

_____

QUESTION 3
When $V = 21$ and $A = 7$.

Answer:

_____

QUESTION 4
When $V = 32$ and $A = 4$.

Answer:

_____

QUESTION 5
When $V = 42$ and $A = 7$.

Answer:

_____

Section B: Voltage drop

Use the following formula to complete the exercises.

Ohm's law

Voltage drop across a resistance when a current is flowing can be calculated using the formula:

$V = IR$ (Ohm's law)

where

V = voltage drop	(unit is volts, V)
I = current	(unit is amps, A)
R = resistance	(unit is ohms, Ω)

Calculate the voltage drop (V) in the questions below.

QUESTION 1
I = 4 amps and R = 3 Ω.

Answer:

_____

QUESTION 2
I = 7 amps and R = 5 Ω.

Answer:

_____

QUESTION 3
I = 4 amps and R = 1.4 Ω.

Answer:

_____

QUESTION 4
I = 12 amps and R = 1.5 Ω.

Answer:

_____

QUESTION 5
I = 6 amps and R = 0.5 Ω.

Answer:

_____

Section C: Electrical power

Short-answer questions

Specific instructions to students

- This section will help you to improve your ability to solve electrical equations by substitution.
- Read the following questions and answer all of them in the spaces provided.
- *You may use a calculator.*
- You need to show all working.

Use the following formula to complete the exercises.

Power formula

The formula used for calculating the power from a supply is:

$$P = \frac{V^2}{R}$$

where

P = power	(unit is watts, W)
V = voltage drop	(unit is volts, V)
R = resistance	(unit is ohms, Ω)

Calculate the value of power in the questions below.

QUESTION 1

$V = 240$ volts and $R = 20\,\Omega$.

Answer:

_____

QUESTION 2

$V = 240$ volts and $R = 15\,\Omega$.

Answer:

_____

QUESTION 3

$V = 12$ volts and $R = 3.5\,\Omega$.

Answer:

_____

QUESTION 4

$V = 12$ volts and $R = 2.5\,\Omega$.

Answer:

_____

QUESTION 5

$V = 12$ volts and $R = 1.5\,\Omega$.

Answer:

_____

Section D: Impedance

Short-answer questions

Specific instructions to students

- This section will help you to improve your ability to solve electrical equations by substitution.
- Read the following questions and answer all of them in the spaces provided.
- *You may use a calculator.*
- You need to show all working.

Use the following formula to complete the exercises:

Impedance in a circuit

To calculate the impedance in a circuit, the following formula can be used:

$$Z = \sqrt{R^2 + X^2}$$

where

Z = impedance	(unit is ohms, Ω)
R = resistance	(unit is ohms, Ω)
X = reactance	(unit is ohms, Ω)

Calculate the value of impedance, correct to two decimal places, in the following questions.

QUESTION 1

$R = 10\,\Omega$ and $X = 12\,\Omega$.

Answer:

_____

QUESTION 2

$R = 8\,\Omega$ and $X = 10.5\,\Omega$.

Answer:

_____

QUESTION 3

$R = 22\,\Omega$ and $X = 25.5\,\Omega$.

Answer:

_____

QUESTION 4

$R = 38\,\Omega$ and $X = 44.5\,\Omega$.

Answer:

_____

QUESTION 5

$R = 56\,\Omega$ and $X = 68.5\,\Omega$.

Answer:

_____

Section A: One-step equations

Rule: Whatever is done to one side of an equation *must* be done to the other side.

Use the following example to answer questions 1 to 5.

EXAMPLE

Solve the equation $y + 3 = 4$

To get y by itself, 3 is subtracted from *both* sides.

$y + 3 - 3 = 4 - 3$

$y + 0 = 1$

$y = 1$

QUESTION 1

Solve the equation $y + 4 = 6$

Answer:

_____

QUESTION 2

Solve the equation $b + 13 = 15$

Answer:

_____

QUESTION 3

Solve the equation $m - 8 = 7$

Answer:

_____

QUESTION 4

Solve the equation $g + 9 = -13$

Answer:

_____

QUESTION 5

Solve the equation $t - 12 = -10$

Answer:

_____

Use the following examples to answer questions 6 to 10.

EXAMPLE

Solve the equation $4n = 12$

To get n by itself, *both* sides are divided by 4.

$\dfrac{4n}{4} = \dfrac{12}{4}$

$n = 3$

EXAMPLE

Solve the equation $\dfrac{e}{3} = 8$

To get e by itself, *both* sides are multiplied by 3.

$3 \times \dfrac{e}{3} = 8 \times 3$

$e = 24$

QUESTION 6

Solve the equation $5j = 35$

Answer:

QUESTION 7

Solve the equation $9f = 108$

Answer:

QUESTION 8

Solve the equation $11t = 121$

Answer:

QUESTION 9

Solve the equation $12a = 72$

Answer:

QUESTION 10

Solve the equation $15r = 225$

Answer:

Section B: Two-step equations

Short-answer questions

Specific instructions to students

- This section is designed to help you to both improve your skills and to increase your speed in solving two-step equations.
- Read the following questions and answer all of them in the spaces provided.
- You may *not* use a calculator.
- You need to show all working.

Use the following example to answer questions 1 to 5.

EXAMPLE

Solve the equation $2m + 2 = 20$.

STEP 1

Subtract 2 from *both* sides to get $2m$ by itself.

$$2m + 2 = 20$$

$$2m + 2 - 2 = 20 - 2$$

$$2m = 18$$

STEP 2

Divide *both* sides by 2 to get m by itself.

$$\frac{2m}{2} = \frac{18}{2}$$

$$m = 9$$

QUESTION 1

Solve the equation $4g + 6 = 10$

Answer:

QUESTION 2

Solve the equation $7v + 7 = 77$

Answer:

QUESTION 3

Solve the equation $9s - 12 = 69$

Answer:

QUESTION 4

Solve the equation $12j - 15 = 129$

Answer:

_____

QUESTION 5

Solve the equation $15i + 15 = 165$

Answer:

_____

Use the following example to answer questions 6 to 10.

EXAMPLE

Solve the equation $\frac{2g}{3} = 6$.

STEP 1

Multiply *both* sides by 3.

$$3 \times \frac{2g}{3} = 18 \times 3$$

$$2g = 18$$

STEP 2

Divide *both* sides by 2 to get g by itself.

$$\frac{2g}{2} = \frac{18}{2}$$

$$g = 9$$

QUESTION 6

Solve the equation $\frac{2m}{3} = 14$

Answer:

_____

QUESTION 7

Solve the equation $\frac{7p}{4} = 14$

Answer:

_____

QUESTION 8

Solve the equation $\frac{10w}{12} = 10$

Answer:

_____

QUESTION 9

Solve the equation $\frac{12k}{6} = 12$

Answer:

_____

QUESTION 10

Solve the equation $\frac{10g}{2} = 17$

Answer:

_____

Use the following example to solve questions 11 to 15.

EXAMPLE

Solve the equation $3(g + 2) = 15$

STEP 1

Divide *both* sides by 3.

$$\frac{3(g + 2)}{3} = \frac{15}{3}$$

$$g + 2 = 5$$

STEP 2

Subtract 2 from *both* sides to get g by itself.

$$g + 2 - 2 = 5 - 2$$

$$g = 3$$

QUESTION 11

Solve the equation $3(f + 8) = 24$

Answer:

_____

QUESTION 12

Solve the equation $7(m + 9) = 56$

Answer:

_____

QUESTION 13

Solve the equation $11(v + 12) = 121$

Answer:

_____

QUESTION 14

Solve the equation $6(n - 18) = 72$

Answer:

_____

QUESTION 15

Solve the equation $10(p - 23) = 110$

Answer:

_____

Use the following example to answer questions 16 to 20.

EXAMPLE

Solve the equation $\dfrac{g + 3}{4} = 5$.

STEP 1

Multiply *both* sides by 4.

$$4 \times \frac{g + 3}{4} = 5 \times 4$$

$$g + 3 = 20$$

STEP 2

Subtract 3 from *both* sides to get g by itself.

$$g + 3 - 3 = 20 - 3$$

$$g = 17$$

QUESTION 16

Solve the equation $\dfrac{k + 6}{3} = 4$

Answer:

_____

QUESTION 17

Solve the equation $\dfrac{n + 12}{8} = 7$

Answer:

_____

QUESTION 18

Solve the equation $\dfrac{2m + 18}{3} = 38$

Answer:

_____

QUESTION 19

Solve the equation $\dfrac{5x - 25}{4} = 100$

Answer:

_____

QUESTION 20

Solve the equation $\dfrac{9y - 20}{2} = 62$

Answer:

_____

Section C: Three-step equations

Use the following example to complete the exercises.

EXAMPLE

Solve the equation $4y - 5 = y + 4$.

STEP 1

Subtract y from *both* sides.

$4y - y - 5 = y - y + 4$

$\qquad 3y - 5 = 4$

STEP 2

Add 5 to *both* sides to get $3y$ by itself.

$3y - 5 + 5 = 4 + 5$

$\qquad 3y = 9$

STEP 3

Divide *both* sides by 3 to get y by itself.

$$\frac{3y}{3} = \frac{9}{3}$$

$\qquad y = 3$

QUESTION 1

Solve the equation $3n - 6 = n + 8$.

Answer:

_____

QUESTION 2

Solve the equation $6g + 2 = 2g + 10$.

Answer:

_____

QUESTION 3

Solve the equation $9f - 3 = 3f + 69$.

Answer:

_____

QUESTION 4

Solve the equation $10v + 13 = -2v + 157$.

Answer:

_____

QUESTION 5

Solve the equation $12m - 44 = -3m + 31$.

Answer:

_____

Section A: One-step transposition

Short-answer questions

Specific instructions to students

- This section is designed to help you to both improve your skills and to increase your speed in transposing formulas.
- Read the following questions below and answer all of them in the spaces provided.
- You may *not* use a calculator.
- You need to show all working.

Watts in a circuit

The formula for calculating the number of watts in a circuit is given as:

$W = VA$

where

W = watts
V = volts
A = amps

This formula may need to be transposed (where the values exchange places) to make a particular value the subject.

For example, to find volts, make V the subject (by dividing both sides of the formula by A).

$$V = \frac{W}{A}$$

The most important consideration when transposing a formula is to make sure that any operation that is completed on one side of the formula must be completed on the other side too.

In the questions below, transpose the formulas for the given subjects.

QUESTION 1

In $T = HK$, make K the subject.

Answer:

QUESTION 2

In $B = QZ$, make Z the subject.

Answer:

QUESTION 3

In $Y = \dfrac{D}{G}$, make D the subject.

Answer:

QUESTION 4

In $PF = XY$, make Y the subject.

Answer:

QUESTION 5

In $JK = MNP$, make N the subject.

Answer:

Section B: Two-step transposition

Use the following example to answer questions 1 to 5.

EXAMPLE

Transpose the formula $g = 2(n - j)$ to make n the subject.

STEP 1

Divide *both* sides by 2.

$$\frac{g}{2} = \frac{2(n - j)}{2}$$

$$\frac{g}{2} = n - j$$

STEP 2

Add j to each side to get n by itself.

$$\frac{g}{2} + j = n$$

In the questions below, transpose the formulas for the given subjects.

QUESTION 1

In $k = 4(h - m)$, make h the subject.

Answer:

_____

QUESTION 2

In $w = 6(2y + 8)$, make y the subject.

Answer:

_____

QUESTION 3

In $2r = 9(3f + 3)$, make f the subject.

Answer:

_____

QUESTION 4

In $3d = 12(5e - 6)$, make e the subject.

Answer:

_____

QUESTION 5

In $6a = 10(12p + 5)$, make p the subject.

Answer:

_____

Use the following example to answer questions 6 to 10.

EXAMPLE

Transpose the formula $a = 3k^2$ to make k the subject.

STEP 1

Divide *both* sides by 3.

$a = 3k^2$

$\dfrac{a}{3} = k^2$

STEP 2

Take the square root of *both* sides.

$\dfrac{\sqrt{a}}{\sqrt{3}} = \sqrt{k^2}$

$\dfrac{\sqrt{a}}{\sqrt{3}} = k$

In the questions below, transpose the formulas for the given subjects.

QUESTION 6

In $m = 4h^2$, make h the subject.

Answer:

_____

QUESTION 7

In $y = 8n^2$, make n the subject.

Answer:

_____

QUESTION 8

In $j = 7r^2$, make r the subject.

Answer:

_____

QUESTION 9

In $f = 12e^2$, make e the subject.

Answer:

_____

QUESTION 10

In $w = 17q^2$, make q the subject.

Answer:

_____

9780170474535

Section A: Ohm's law

Ohm's law

In any electrical circuit, the current is directly proportional to the voltage and inversely proportional to the circuit resistance.
As an equation, this is expressed as

$$I = \frac{V}{R}$$

where

I = current	(unit is amps, A)
V = potential difference	(unit is volts, V)
R = resistance	(unit is ohms, Ω)

Using transpositions of Ohm's law, answer each of the questions below.

QUESTION 1

Find I when V = 12 volts and R = 4 Ω.

Answer:

_____

QUESTION 2

Find I when V = 24 volts and R = 6 Ω.

Answer:

_____

QUESTION 3

Make R the subject and solve given that V = 14 volts and I = 2.5 amps.

Answer:

_____

QUESTION 4

Make V the subject and solve given that I = 16 amps and R = 20 Ω.

Answer:

_____

QUESTION 5

Make I the subject and solve given that V = 12.5 volts and R = 4.5 Ω.

Answer:

_____

Section B: Electrical power in a circuit

Formula for power

A formula that can be used to calculate the power in an electrical circuit is given as:

$P = I^2 R$

where

P = power	(unit is watts, W)
I = current	(unit is amps, A)
R = resistance	(unit is ohms, Ω)

Solve the following by substituting in values and/or transposing the formula for power.

QUESTION 1

Find P when $I = 0.5$ amps and $R = 20\,\Omega$.

Answer:

_____

QUESTION 2

Find P when $I = 1.5$ amps and $R = 30\,\Omega$.

Answer:

_____

QUESTION 3

Make R the subject and solve given that $P = 4.5$ watts and $I = 1.5$ amps.

Answer:

_____

QUESTION 4

Make I the subject and solve given that $R = 36\,\Omega$ and $P = 9.5$ watts.

Answer:

_____

QUESTION 5

Find P when $I = 3.5$ amps and $R = 65\,\Omega$.

Answer:

_____

Section C: Resistance in a series circuit

Worded practical problems

Specific instructions to students

- This unit is designed to help you to both improve your skills and to increase your speed in calculating the unknowns in electrical formulas.
- Read the following questions below and answer all of them in the spaces provided.
- You may *not* use a calculator.
- You need to show all working.

Resistance in a series circuit

The value in ohms of individual resistors in any series is added together to determine what the final resistance is. The formula that is used to work out the total resistance to current flow in any series is given as:

$R_{Total} = R_1 + R_2 + R_3 + \ldots$

Three resistors are in series in a circuit. $R_1 = 5\,\Omega$, $R_2 = 15\,\Omega$ and $R_3 = 50\,\Omega$.

Hence,

$R_{Total} = R_1 + R_2 + R_3$
$= 5\,\Omega + 15\,\Omega + 50\,\Omega$
$= 70\,\Omega$ (total resistance)

Answer the following questions using the values given.

QUESTION 1

Solve for R_{Total} given that $R_1 = 3.5\,\Omega$, $R_2 = 6.5\,\Omega$ and $R_3 = 8.5\,\Omega$.

Answer:

_____

QUESTION 2

Solve for R_{Total} given that $R_1 = 15.5\,\Omega$, $R_2 = 23.5\,\Omega$, $R_3 = 31.5\,\Omega$ and $R_4 = 56.5\,\Omega$.

Answer:

_____

QUESTION 3

Solve for R_3 given that $R_{Total} = 55\,\Omega$, $R_1 = 12\,\Omega$, $R_2 = 11\,\Omega$ and $R_4 = 16\,\Omega$.

Answer:

_____

QUESTION 4

Solve for R_2 given that $R_{Total} = 125\,\Omega$, $R_1 = 11.5\,\Omega$, $R_3 = 9.5\,\Omega$ and $R_4 = 7.5\,\Omega$.

Answer:

_____

QUESTION 5

Solve for R_4 given that $R_{Total} = 465\,\Omega$, $R_1 = 9.8\,\Omega$, $R_2 = 6.6\,\Omega$ and $R_3 = 14.8\,\Omega$.

Answer:

_____

Section D: AC circuits

Impedance formula

In AC (alternating current) circuits, resistance, reactance and impedance can all be calculated by using Pythagoras' theorem. The formula for Pythagoras' theorem is given as:

$A^2 + B^2 = C^2$ or it can also be written as:

$C^2 = A^2 + B^2$

When applied in an electrical context, the values are changed, but the structure of the formula remains the same, thus giving:

$Z^2 = R^2 + X^2$

where

Z = impedance	(unit is ohms, Ω)
R = resistance	(unit is ohms, Ω)
X = reactance	(unit is ohms, Ω)

Solve the following questions using the values given, correct to two decimal places.

QUESTION 1

Find Z given that $R = 17\,\Omega$ and $X = 13\,\Omega$.

Answer:

_____

QUESTION 2

Find Z given that $R = 45\,\Omega$ and $X = 38\,\Omega$.

Answer:

_____

QUESTION 3

Make R the subject and solve given that $X = 6\,\Omega$ and $Z = 12\,\Omega$.

Answer:

_____

QUESTION 4

Make X the subject and solve given that $R = 6.2\,\Omega$ and $Z = 15.6\,\Omega$.

Answer:

_____

QUESTION 5

Find Z given that $R = 15.5\,\Omega$ and $X = 11.5\,\Omega$.

Answer:

_____

Section A: Converting decimals to percentages

Short-answer questions

Specific instructions to students

- This section is designed to help you to both improve your skills and to increase your speed in converting decimals to percentages.
- Read the following questions below and answer all of them in the spaces provided.
- You may *not* use a calculator.
- You need to show all working.

EXAMPLE

Convert 0.5 to a percentage.

Move the decimal place *two places* to the *right* or multiply the number by 100.

$0.5 \times 100 = 50\%$

In the questions below, convert the decimal to a percentage by following the example given above.

QUESTION 1

$0.8 =$

Answer:

_____

QUESTION 2

$0.75 =$

Answer:

_____

QUESTION 3

$0.05 =$

Answer:

_____

QUESTION 4

$0.002 =$

Answer:

_____

QUESTION 5

$1.7 =$

Answer:

_____

Section B: Converting fractions to percentages

EXAMPLE

Convert $\dfrac{1}{2}$ to a percentage.

$$\dfrac{1}{2} \times \dfrac{100}{1} = \dfrac{100}{2}$$
$$= 50\%$$

In the questions below, convert the fractions to percentages, correct to one decimal place, by following the example given above.

QUESTION 1

$\dfrac{1}{3} =$

Answer:

_____

QUESTION 2

$\dfrac{1}{5} =$

Answer:

_____

QUESTION 3

$\dfrac{2}{7} =$

Answer:

_____

QUESTION 4

$\dfrac{4}{9} =$

Answer:

_____

QUESTION 5

$\dfrac{35}{40} =$

Answer:

_____

Section C: Practical problems using the conversion of numbers to percentages

Answer the following questions correct to one decimal place.

QUESTION 1

Out of a packet of 12 resistors, two are found to be defective. What is this as a percentage?

Answer:

QUESTION 2

An electrical company produces capacitors and of the 1200 that are made, 36 are found to be defective. What percentage are defective?

Answer:

QUESTION 3

Eleven out of 250 multimeters are found to have faults or are inaccurate. What is this as a percentage?

Answer:

QUESTION 4

Seven out of 360 voltage sticks are found to have defects. What is this as a percentage?

Answer:

QUESTION 5

Two out of 16 electrical converters are defective. What is this as a percentage?

Answer:

Section A: Efficiency

Electrical efficiency

You can calculate the electrical efficiency of electrical devices by using the formula:

$$\text{Efficiency} = \frac{\text{power output}}{\text{power input}} \times 100$$

EXAMPLE

A mechanical device has a power input of 80 W and a power output of 60 W. Calculate the efficiency of the device.

$$\text{Efficiency} = \frac{60}{80} \times 100 = 75\%$$

In the questions below, find the efficiency of each of the devices, correct to one decimal place, using the information given.

QUESTION 1

A radiator has a power output of 950 W and a power input of 1000 W.

Answer:

_____

QUESTION 2

An electric motor has a power output of 3.5 kW and a power input of 3.75 kW.

Answer:

_____

QUESTION 3

An electric motor has a power output of 2 kW and a power input of 2.25 kW.

Answer:

_____

QUESTION 4

An amplifier has a power output of 220 W and a power input of 225 W.

Answer:

_____

QUESTION 5

A radiator has a power output of 750 W and a power input of 900 W.

Answer:

_____

Section B: Voltage

Short-answer questions

Specific instructions to students

- This section is designed to help you to both improve your skills and to increase your speed in calculating total voltage.
- Read the following questions below and answer all of them in the spaces provided.
- You may *not* use a calculator.
- You need to show all working.

EXAMPLE

The voltage of a circuit is 240 V. The voltage drops by 3% at the end of the circuit. Calculate the total voltage after the 3% drop.

Voltage drop $= \dfrac{3}{100} \times 240 = 7.2\,\text{V}$

Total voltage $= 240\,\text{V} - 7.2\,\text{V} = 232.8\,\text{V}$

Solve the following questions using the example given above.

QUESTION 1

The voltage of a circuit is 240 V. The voltage drops by 5% at the end of the circuit. Calculate the total voltage after the 5% drop.

Answer:

_____

QUESTION 2

The voltage of a circuit is 240 V. The voltage drops by 8% at the end of the circuit. Calculate the total voltage after the 8% drop.

Answer:

_____

QUESTION 3

A resistor has a value of 35 Ω ± 5%. What is the maximum and minimum value of the resistor?

Answer:

_____

_____

QUESTION 4

A resistor has a value of 1500 Ω ± 10%. What is the maximum and minimum value of the resistor?

Answer:

_____

_____

QUESTION 5

A resistor has a value of 18 500 Ω ± 10%. What is the maximum and minimum value of the resistor?

Answer:

_____

_____

Section C: Percentage of error

Short-answer questions

Specific instructions to students

- This section is designed to help you to both improve your skills and to increase your speed in calculating the percentage of error.
- Read the following questions below and answer all of them in the spaces provided.
- *You may use a calculator.*
- You need to show all working.

EXAMPLE

Calculate the percentage of error if a calculated value is found to be 100 V and the corresponding measured value is 104 V.

$$\% \text{ error} = \frac{\text{difference}}{\text{calculated value}} \times 100$$

$$= \frac{104 - 100}{100} \times 100$$

$$= \frac{4}{100} \times 100$$

$$= 4\%$$

Calculate the percentage of error in the following scenarios, correct to two decimal places, using the given formula.

QUESTION 1

The voltage in a particular circuit is measured at 80 V; however, the voltage should be 85 V.

Answer:

QUESTION 2

The voltage in a particular circuit is measured at 137 V; however, the voltage should be 144 V.

Answer:

QUESTION 3

The voltage in a particular circuit is measured at 3.45 kW; however, the voltage should be 3.48 kW.

Answer:

QUESTION 4

The resistance in a circuit is measured at 48.5 Ω; however, the resistance should be 51 Ω.

Answer:

QUESTION 5

The resistance in a circuit is 21 500 Ω; however, the voltage should be 22 750 Ω.

Answer:

9780170474535

Unit 16: Trigonometry

Section A: An introduction

Trigonometric formulas

The sides of a right-angled triangle are named in relation to where the angle is inside the triangle.
Opposite is the side opposite to where the angle is given.
Adjacent is the side that is 'next to' the angle that is given.
Hypotenuse is the longest side of the triangle.
There are three functions that can express a ratio of the length of one side to another side. These are sine, cosine and tangent, also known as sin, cos and tan.

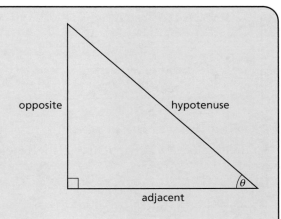

The following rules can be applied to the above triangle.

Rule 1	Rule 2	Rule 3
$\sin \theta = \dfrac{\text{opposite}}{\text{hypotenuse}}$	$\cos \theta = \dfrac{\text{adjacent}}{\text{hypotenuse}}$	$\tan \theta = \dfrac{\text{opposite}}{\text{adjacent}}$

Use a scientific calculator to calculate the following values correct to four decimal places.

QUESTION 1

$\sin 15° =$

Answer:

_____

QUESTION 2

$\cos 15° =$

Answer:

_____

QUESTION 3

$\tan 15° =$

Answer:

_____

QUESTION 4

$\sin 30° =$

Answer:

_____

QUESTION 5

$\cos 30° =$

Answer:

_____

QUESTION 6

$\tan 30° =$

Answer:

_____

Section B: Sine (sin), cosine (cos), tangent (tan)

EXAMPLE

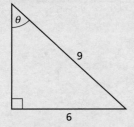

Find the value of θ in the right-angled triangle above.

STEP 1

Work out the formula to use.

We have the hypotenuse and the side opposite to the angle, and we need to find the angle.

So use sine.

STEP 2

Write out the formula with the values in it.

$$\sin \theta = \frac{\text{opposite}}{\text{hypotenuse}}$$

$$= \frac{6}{9}$$

$$= 0.6666$$

STEP 3

Find the value of θ by using inverse sine.

On your calculator, press 'sin^{-1}' (which is usually 'SHIFT' followed by 'sin'). Then enter the number, in this case: 0.6666.

$$\theta = \sin^{-1}(0.666)$$

$$= 41.81°$$

Use sin θ, cos θ or tan θ to find the value of the unknown angle in the following right-angled triangles, correct to two decimal places.

QUESTION 1

Answer:

_____

QUESTION 2

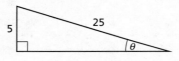

Answer:

_____

QUESTION 3

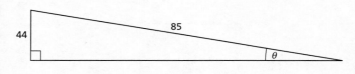

Answer:

_____

QUESTION 4

20   18

θ

Answer:

_____

QUESTION 5

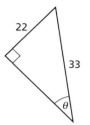

22

33

θ

Answer:

_____

QUESTION 6

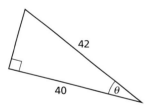

42

40   θ

Answer:

_____

QUESTION 7

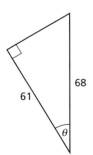

68

61

θ

Answer:

_____

QUESTION 8

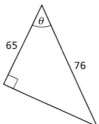

θ

65   76

Answer:

_____

QUESTION 9

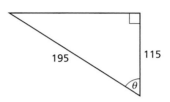

195   115

θ

Answer:

_____

QUESTION 10

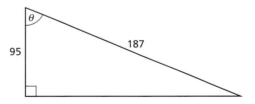

θ

95   187

Answer:

_____

QUESTION 11

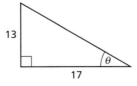

13

17   θ

Answer:

_____

QUESTION 12

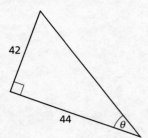

Answer:

_____

QUESTION 13

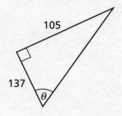

Answer:

_____

QUESTION 14

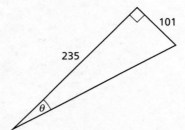

Answer:

_____

QUESTION 15

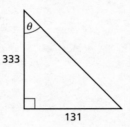

Answer:

_____

9780170474535

Section C: Finding an unknown side

EXAMPLE

Find y in the following right-angled triangle by transposing a trigonometric formula that you have chosen to solve the problem.

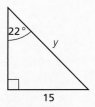

STEP 1

Work out the formula to use.

We have an angle and a side opposite to it, and we need to find the hypotenuse.

So use sine.

STEP 2

Write out the formula with the values in it.

$$\sin \theta = \frac{\text{opposite}}{\text{hypotenuse}}$$

$$\sin 22° = \frac{15}{y}$$

STEP 3

To find y, you need to transpose the formula.

$$y = \frac{15}{\sin 22°}$$

STEP 4

Work out $\sin 22°$ on your calculator, then divide 15 by this number.

$$y = \frac{15}{0.3746}$$

$$= 40.04$$

Using either sin, cos or tan, solve the following by finding a value for the unknown side, correct to two decimal places.

QUESTION 1

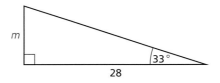

Answer:

_____

QUESTION 2

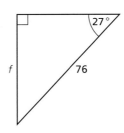

Answer:

_____

QUESTION 3

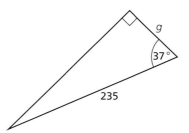

Answer:

_____

QUESTION 4

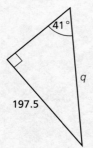

Answer:

_____

QUESTION 5

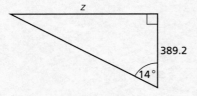

Answer:

_____

QUESTION 6

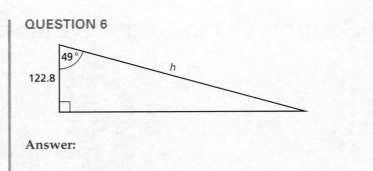

Answer:

_____

Unit 17: Perimeter, Area and Estimation

> **Perimeter of a rectangle**
>
> Perimeter is the length of all sides added together.
> Perimeter = length + breadth + length + breadth
> $P = l + b + l + b$
>
> **Area of a rectangle**
>
> Area = length × breadth and is given in square units
> $A = l \times b$

QUESTION 1

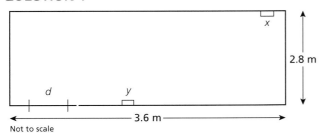

Not to scale

Calculate the perimeter (P) and area (A) of the room. The room is to be fitted with two power outlets (x and y). Estimate the distance to each power outlet of the room from the door, d, given the dimensions of the room.

Answer:

_____

_____

_____

_____

QUESTION 2

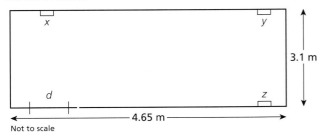

Not to scale

Calculate the perimeter (P) and area (A) of the room. Estimate the distance to power outlets: x, y and z from the door, d, given the dimensions of the room.

Answer:

_____

_____

_____

_____

_____

_____

QUESTION 3

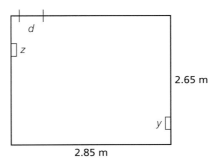

Not to scale

Calculate the perimeter (P) and area (A) of the room. Estimate the distance to power outlets: x and y from the door, d, given the dimensions of the room.

Answer:

_____

_____

_____

_____

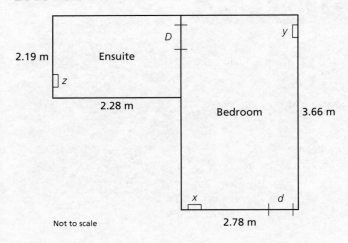

Calculate the perimeter (*P*) and area (*A*) of each room. Estimate the distance to power outlets x and y from door d, and the distance from power outlet z to door D, given the dimensions of the rooms.

Answer:

_____

_____

_____

_____

_____

_____

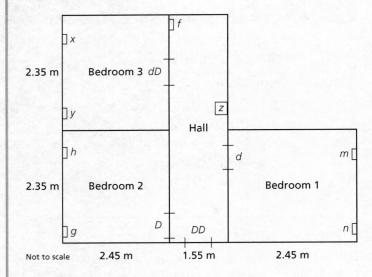

Calculate the perimeter (*P*) and area (*A*) of each space.

Given the dimensions of the spaces, estimate the following distances.

- To power outlet m from door d.
- To power outlet n from door d.
- To power outlet g from door D.
- To power outlet h from door D.
- To power outlet x from door dD.
- To power outlet y from door dD.
- To power outlet z from door DD.
- To power outlet f from door DD.

Answer:

_____

_____

_____

_____

_____

_____

_____

_____

_____

_____

_____

_____

_____

Unit 18: Tables and Graphs

Section A: An introduction

An important skill in the electrical trade is the ability to read, interpret and understand tables and graphs. Many tables and graphs are used to present data and information related to current, power, carrying capacity of devices and appliances, etc.

QUESTION 1

Arrange the following electrical appliances in order of the amount of power (watts) that each uses.

Microwave	650 watts
Stereo	200 watts
Bedside clock	2 watts
Dishwasher	2400 watts
Strip heater	2000 watts
Vacuum cleaner	750 watts
Kettle	1500 watts

Answer:

QUESTION 2

Which electrical appliance uses the *most* amount of power?

Answer:

QUESTION 3

Which electrical appliance uses the *least* amount of power?

Answer:

QUESTION 4

Why would the electrical appliance that uses the *most* power need a lot of power?

Answer:

QUESTION 5

What factors could influence the amount of power that is used by an electrical appliance?

Answer:

QUESTION 6

What could be done to reduce the amount of power used by an electrical appliance?

Answer:

Section B: Reading and interpreting tables

Short-answer questions

Specific instructions to students

- This section is designed to help you to both improve your skills and to increase your speed in reading and interpreting tables
- Read the following questions below and answer all of them in the spaces provided.
- You may *not* use a calculator.
- You need to show all working.

Information can be represented in tables and electricians need to be able to read, analyse, understand and interpret tables. Different types of tables are used to represent different types of data.

QUESTION 1

Explain the correlation between resistance and temperature in the table below.

Table 1: Copper wire – resistance vs temperature

Temperature (°C)	Resistance in ohms (Ω)
20	100.00 Ω
21	100.38 Ω
22	100.76 Ω
23	101.14 Ω
24	101.52 Ω
25	101.90 Ω
26	102.28 Ω

Answer:

_____

_____

QUESTION 2

Read and interpret what the data represents in the table below.

Table 2: Australian vehicle trailer wiring standards

	Circuit	Circuit conductor	Circuit conductor colour
7-pin connector	1	Left-hand turn	Yellow
	2	Reversing signal	Black
	3	Earth return	White
	4	Right-hand turn	Green
	5	Service brakes	Blue
	6	Stop lamps	Red
	7	Rear lamps, clearance and side marker lamps	Brown
12-pin connector	8	Battery charger/ electric winch	Orange
	9	Auxiliaries, etc./ battery feed	Pink
	10	Earth return	White
	11	Rear fog lamp	Grey
	12	Spare	Violet

Answer:

_____

_____

_____

_____

QUESTION 3

Use the data in the table below to plot a graph of 'Voltage versus Charge' in AGM and Wet cell. Use the blank grid below the table to plot your graph.

Table 3: Voltage indicating battery charge left

Charge (%)	AGM (V)	Wet cell (V)
100	12.9	12.75
90	12.8	12.7
80	12.6	12.55
70	12.4	12.3
60	12.2	12
50	12.1	11.85
40	12	11.7
30	11.9	11.65
20	11.7	11.55
10	11.3	11.32
0	11	10.8

Answer:

Voltage versus Charge

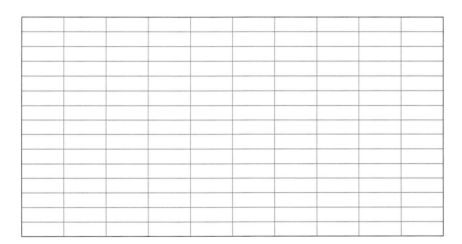

QUESTION 4

Analyse and interpret what is happening in the graph you have plotted for Question 3 as the voltage from the battery charges.

Answer:

_____

_____

QUESTION 5

Analyse the table below and write a brief description of the relation between an increase in amps compared to the length and gauge of wire needed.

Table 4: Feeder wire size chart

Amps at 12 volts	Length of wire (cm)						
0 to 1	100 cm	150 cm	200 cm	300 cm	450 cm	600 cm	750 cm
1.5	18	18	18	18	18	18	18
2	18	18	18	18	18	18	18
3	18	18	18	18	18	18	18
4	18	18	18	18	18	18	18
5	18	18	18	18	18	18	18
6	18	18	18	18	18	18	16
7	18	18	18	18	18	18	16
8	18	18	18	18	18	18	16
9	18	18	18	18	18	18	14
10	18	18	18	18	16	16	14
11	18	18	18	18	16	16	14
12	18	18	18	18	16	16	14
15	18	18	18	18	14	14	12
18	18	18	16	16	14	14	12
20	18	18	16	16	14	12	10
22	18	18	16	14	12	12	10
24	18	18	16	14	12	12	10
30	18	16	14	14	10	10	10
36	18	14	14	12	10	10	10
40	18	14	12	12	10	10	6
50	18	14	12	10	10	10	6
100	18	12	10	10	6	6	4
150	18	10	8	8	4	4	2
200	18	8	8	8	4	4	2

Answer:

_____

_____

_____

Table 5: Minimum separation of aerial customer cabling, including joint or termination enclosures and telecommunications poles or structures, from aerial power lines and fittings

Type of power line, structure or fitting		At a shared/ common pole or structure	In span	Telecommunications pole or structure		
				Crossing		Separate parallel route
				Horiz.	Radial	
Light fitting, stay fitting or power conduit at a pole		50 mm	n/a	n/a		n/a
LV cable independently secured to the same catenary support as the customer cable		50 mm or insulating conduit	Insulating conduit	n/a		n/a
Independently supported, insulated LV		0.6 m	0.6 m	2.4 m	2.4 m	2.4 m
Uninsulated LV		1.2 m	0.6 m	2.4 m	2.4 m	10 m
HV	≤ 11 kV	2.4 m	1.2 m	2.4 m	3.7 m	10 m
	> 11 kV ≤ 33 kV		2.1 m	2.4 m	4.0 m	10 m
	> 33 kV ≤ 66 kV	3.0 m	2.1 m	2.4 m	4.0 m	10 m
	> 66 kV ≤ 132 kV		3.0 m	2.4 m	4.6 m	10 m
	> 132 kV ≤ 220 kV		3.7 m	2.4 m	6.0 m	10 m
	> 220 kV ≤ 330 kV		4.6 m	2.4 m	7.5 m	10 m
	> 330 kV					50 m

Australian Standard (AS/CA S009:2013), Installation Requirements for Customer Cabling (Wiring Rules) © Communications Alliance Ltd

Using the table above, answer the following questions.

a For an independently supported power line, structure or fitting, insulated LV, what is the in span value?

Answer:

_____

b For an uninsulated LV power line, structure or fitting, what is the value for a separate parallel route of a telecommunications pole or structure?

Answer:

_____

c For an HV power line, structure or fitting of > 33 kV ≤ 66 kV, what is the in span value?

Answer:

_____

d For a HV power line, structure or fitting of > 132 kV < 220 kV, what is the in span value?

Answer:

_____

e For a light fitting, stay fitting or power conduit at a shared/common pole or structure, what is the minimum separation value?

Answer:

_____

Section C: Reading and interpreting graphs

Short-answer questions

Specific instructions to students

- This section is designed to help you to both improve your skills and to increase your speed in reading and interpreting graphs.
- Read the questions below and answer all of them in the spaces provided.
- You may *not* use a calculator.
- You need to show all working.

The role of graphs is an important one as they offer a different way of representing and interpreting data.

EXAMPLE

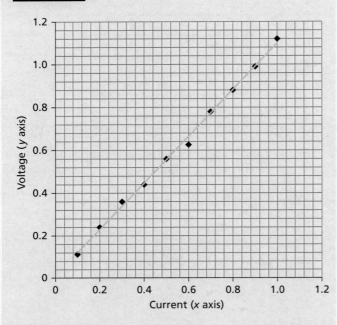

The line graph above has two axes, *x* and *y*. The *x*-axis represents current while the *y*-axis represents voltage. As the current increases, so does the voltage at a similar rate.

Read and interpret the following graphs and explain what is happening in each situation.

QUESTION 1

Graph 1: Solar panel output

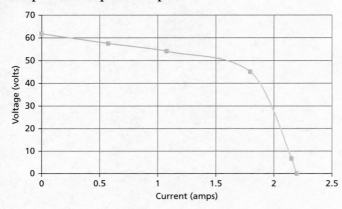

Answer:

_____

_____

_____

_____

_____

_____

QUESTION 2

Graph 2: Resistance graphs

A resistor at constant temperature   A filament lamp   A diode

Answer:

_____

_____

_____

_____

_____

_____

_____

_____

_____

_____

_____

Graph 3: Household electrical usage

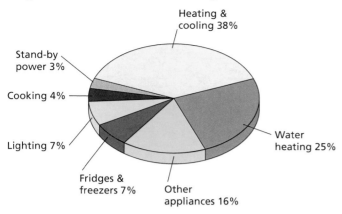

Answer:

_____

_____

_____

_____

_____

QUESTION 4

Graph 4: South Australia − average power demand for summer months December to January, and the effect of increased use of rooftop solar in 2013 and 2014

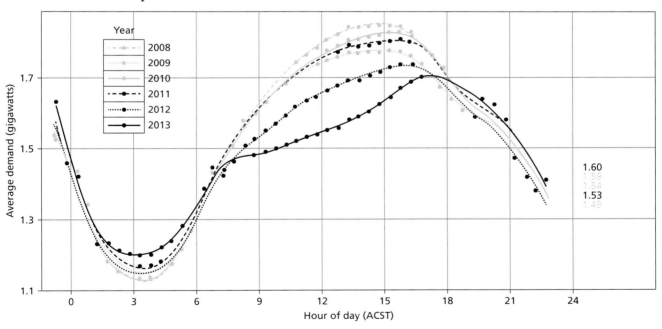

© Mike Sandiford

Answer:

_____

_____

_____

_____

Graph 5: Light globes ranked by power consumption

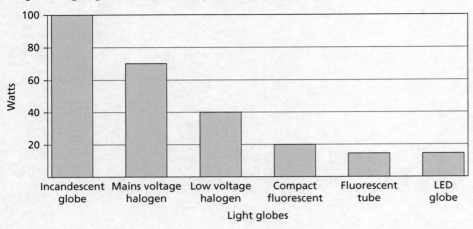

Answer:

_____

_____

    9780170474535

Electrical
Practice Written Exam for the Electrical Trade

Reading time: 10 minutes
Writing time: 1 hour 30 minutes

Section A: Literacy
Section B: General Mathematics
Section C: Trade Mathematics

QUESTION and ANSWER BOOK

Section	Topic	Number of questions	Marks
A	Literacy	7	22
B	General Mathematics	11	24
C	Trade Mathematics	46	54
		Total 64	Total 100

The sections may be completed in the order of your choice.
NO CALCULATORS are to be used during the exam for
Section B or up to Section C: Impedance.
CALCULATORS can be used onwards from Section C: Impedance.

Spelling

Read the passage below, and then underline the 20 spelling errors.

10 marks

Walid, Hudson and Justin are talking about electramotive force, also known as emf, during a trainning class. Walid said, 'Did you know that the voltege produced by a sourse of electrical energy, such as a batery, is known as emf? It can be defined as the electrical potantial for any source in a specafic circuit'. 'Wow!' said Hudson. 'How do they work?' Walid explains, 'The electromotive forses have the ability to convert chemical, meckanical, and other forms of energy into electrical energy'.

'Is that the same for batteries?' inqures Hudson. Walid answers, 'With a battery, the charge seperation that helps to produce a voltage diference between the termanals is possible because chemical reactions occur at the electrodes. The electrades are able to convert chemical potential energy into electromaggnetic potential energy'. Justin adds, 'As for electrical genarators, a time-varying magnetic field that is inside the generator generates an electric feald by electromagnetic indaction. This then allows for a voltage difference between the generator terminals to be prodused'.

Fix the spelling errors by writing them out with the correct spelling below.

_____

_____

_____

_____

Alphabetising

Put the following words into alphabetical order.

Ohm's law	Power
Resistance	Watts
Impedance	Amperes
Voltage	Ohms
Proportional	Nano
Current	Giga
Electricity	Mega

_____

_____

_____

_____

_____

_____

_____

_____

_____

_____

_____

_____

_____

_____

Comprehension

Short-answer questions

Specific instructions to students

- Read the following passage and answer the questions using full sentences.

Electricians must carry out a risk assessment in order to determine how likely it is that someone will be exposed to an electrical hazard and what might happen if they are. A risk assessment can help to determine the nature and extent of an electrical risk, whether or not existing control measures are sufficient and effective, what action(s) should be taken to address an electrical risk and how urgently the action(s) need to be taken.

To evaluate the risk associated with electrical threats, it is important to ask: What could happen if the electrical hazard is not tended to? What is the possible effect of the hazard? Are people exposed to the hazard, and if so, how many? Is the hazard likely to cause anyone harm? Could the hazard occur at any time? Other factors that may affect the likelihood of a hazard occurring may include the environment and working conditions that the electrical equipment is being used in, the work habits of the operator and the capability, skill and experience of relevant workers.

Once a hazard has been identified and the risks have been assessed, measures need to be put in place to control the risk. It is important that the correct control is chosen in order to eliminate risk and address the hazard. The first and most effective control measure is elimination. This acts to eliminate the hazard or the harmful work practice. Another control measure is substitution. This involves replacing a hazardous process or material with one that is less hazardous, which will reduce the hazard. The third control measure is known as isolation. This measure prevents anyone from coming into contact with the source of an electrical hazard.

QUESTION 1	1 mark

What does the term 'risk assessment' mean?

Answer:

_____

_____

_____

_____

_____

QUESTION 2	1 mark

What can a risk assessment help to determine?

Answer:

_____

_____

_____

_____

_____

_____

QUESTION 3   1 mark

Are there any other factors that may affect the likelihood of a hazard occurring?

Answer:

_____

_____

_____

_____

QUESTION 4   1 mark

How can the risk of a hazard be controlled?

Answer:

_____

_____

_____

QUESTION 5   1 mark

Name three different types of control measures and briefly explain how each works.

Answer:

_____

_____

_____

_____

_____

_____

_____

_____

_____

_____

Section B: General Mathematics

QUESTION 1   1 + 1 + 1 = 3 marks

What unit of measurement would you use to measure the following? Write the symbol for each measurement.

a   Voltage

Answer:

_____

b   Amount of power

Answer:

_____

c   Resistance

Answer:

_____

QUESTION 2   1 + 1 + 1 = 3 marks

Give examples of where the following might be used in the electrical industry.

a   Percentage

Answer:

_____

b   Decimals

Answer:

_____

c   Formulas

Answer:

_____

QUESTION 3   1 + 1 = 2 marks

Convert the following units.

a   1 kW to watts

Answer:

_____

b   1500 mm to m

Answer:

_____

QUESTION 4   1 + 1 = 2 marks

Estimate the following.

a $101\,\Omega \times 81\,\Omega$

Answer:

___

b $399\,W \times 21\,W$

Answer:

___

QUESTION 5   2 marks

Write the following in descending order.

0.7   0.71   7.1   70.1   701.00   7.0

Answer:

___

QUESTION 6   1 + 1 = 2 marks

Collect like terms and simplify the following.

a $2m + 7 + 4m - 2$

Answer:

___

b $4g - 3 - 9g + 7 - g$

Answer:

___

QUESTION 7   1 + 1 = 2 marks

Round the following numbers to two (2) decimal places.

a   5.177

Answer:

___

b   12.655

Answer:

___

QUESTION 8   1 + 1 = 2 marks

Expand the brackets and solve the following.

a $3(a - 8) + 5(2a - 11)$

Answer:

___

b $13(2x + 8) - 9(3x - 12)$

Answer:

___

QUESTION 9   1 + 1 = 2 marks

Subtract the following:

a $987\,\Omega$ from $1133\,\Omega$

Answer:

___

b $5556\,W$ from $9223\,W$

Answer:

___

QUESTION 10   1 + 1 = 2 marks

Solve the following.

a $4824 \div 3 =$

Answer:

___

b $84.2 \div 0.4 =$

Answer:

___

QUESTION 11   1 + 1 = 2 marks

Using BODMAS, solve the following.

a $(3 \times 7) \times 4 + 9 - 5$

Answer:

___

b $(8 \times 12) \times 2 + 8 - 4$

Answer:

___

Section C: Trade Mathematics

Algebra

Addition

QUESTION 1   1 mark
Simplify $14h + 16 + 27h + 47$

Answer:

_____

QUESTION 2   1 mark
Simplify $39f + 107 + 78f + 398 + 11f$

Answer:

_____

Subtraction

QUESTION 1   1 mark
Simplify $-15t - 6 - 55t - 8$

Answer:

_____

QUESTION 2   1 mark
Simplify $-106m - 34 - 276m - 56$

Answer:

_____

Multiplication

QUESTION 1   1 mark
Simplify $6f \times 3$

Answer:

_____

QUESTION 2   1 mark
Simplify $4(8g + 7)$

Answer:

_____

Division

QUESTION 1   1 mark
Simplify $\dfrac{56c}{8}$

Answer:

_____

QUESTION 2   1 mark
Simplify $\dfrac{15g}{5} + \dfrac{42g}{7}$

Answer:

_____

Exponents (Powers)

QUESTION 1   1 mark
Simplify $5a^2 + 3a - 3a^2 + 7a - 4$

Answer:

_____

QUESTION 2   1 mark
Simplify $11k^2 + 9z^3 - 5k^2 + 7z^3 + k - z + 19$

Answer:

_____

Solving Electrical Equations by Substitution

QUESTION 1   1 mark

Solve $w - 29$, when $w = 11$

Answer:

_____

QUESTION 2   1 mark

Solve $119 + h$, when $h = 89$

Answer:

_____

Voltage drop

QUESTION 1   1 mark

Find V when $I = 65\,A$ and $R = 1.5\,\Omega$.

Answer:

_____

QUESTION 2   1 mark

Find I when $V = 12\,V$ and $R = 2.5\,\Omega$.

Answer:

_____

Electrical power

QUESTION 1   1 mark

Calculate the electrical power from a supply if the voltage is 12 V and the resistance is 12 Ω.

Answer:

_____

QUESTION 2   1 mark

Calculate the electrical power from a supply if the voltage is 24 V and the resistance is 10 Ω.

Answer:

_____

Impedance

(Note: you may use calculators from this point onwards.)

QUESTION 1   1 mark

Calculate the impedance of a circuit that has the following values:

$R = 3\,\Omega$ and $X = 5\,\Omega$.

Answer:

_____

QUESTION 2   1 mark

Calculate the impedance of a circuit that has the following values:

$R = 8\,\Omega$ and $X = 12\,\Omega$.

Answer:

_____

Solving Algebraic Equations

QUESTION 1   1 mark

Solve for m: $m - 12 = 9$

Answer:

_____

QUESTION 2   1 mark

Solve for g: $6(g + 9) = 108$

Answer:

_____

Transposing Formulas

QUESTION 1   1 mark

Make N the subject in $F = HN$.

Answer:

_____

QUESTION 2   1 mark

Make a the subject in $w = \dfrac{5(3a + 12)}{6}$.

Answer:

_____

Working with Electrical Formulas

QUESTION 1   1 mark

Use Ohm's law to find I when $V = 12\,\text{V}$ and $R = 4\,\Omega$.

Answer:

_____

QUESTION 2   1 mark

Make R the subject in Ohm's law and find its value when $V = 16\,\text{V}$ and $I = 3.5\,\text{A}$.

Answer:

_____

Electrical power in a circuit

QUESTION 1   1 mark

Calculate the electrical power (P) in a circuit when $I = 2.5\,\text{A}$ and $R = 20\,\Omega$.

Answer:

_____

QUESTION 2   1 mark

Calculate the electrical power (P) in a circuit when $I = 3.5\,\text{A}$ and $R = 45\,\Omega$.

Answer:

_____

Resistance in a series circuit

QUESTION 1   1 mark

Solve for R_{Total} given that $R_1 = 13.5\,\Omega$, $R_2 = 27.5\,\Omega$, $R_3 = 38.5\,\Omega$ and $R_4 = 55.5\,\Omega$.

Answer:

_____

QUESTION 2   1 mark

Solve for R_4 given that $R_{Total} = 323\,\Omega$; $R_1 = 29.8\,\Omega$, $R_2 = 76.6\,\Omega$ and $R_3 = 114.8\,\Omega$.

Answer:

_____

AC circuits

QUESTION 1   1 mark

Use $Z^2 = R^2 + X^2$ to find Z given that $R = 25\,\Omega$ and $X = 33\,\Omega$.

Answer:

_____

QUESTION 2   1 mark

Use $Z^2 = R^2 + X^2$ to find Z given that $R = 32.5\,\Omega$ and $X = 45.5\,\Omega$.

Answer:

_____

Percentages and Conversions

Convert 0.05 to a percentage.

Answer:

_____

Convert 1.65 to a percentage.

Answer:

_____

Efficiency

Calculate the efficiency of a radiator that has a power output of 980 W and a power input of 1000 W.

Answer:

_____

If an amplifier has a power output of 220 W and a power input of 225 W, calculate its efficiency.

Answer:

_____

Percentage of error

The voltage in a circuit is measured at 90 V, however, the voltage should be 95 V. What is the percentage of error?

_____

The resistance in a circuit is measured at 39.5 Ω, however, the resistance should be 43 Ω. What is the percentage of error?

Answer:

_____

Trigonometry

Find the value of θ in the triangle below.

Answer:

_____

Find the value of θ in the triangle below.

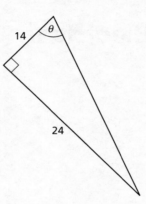

Answer:

_____

Finding an unknown side

Find the value of x in the triangle below.

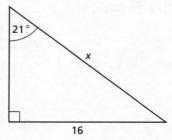

Answer:

_____

_____

QUESTION 2   1 mark

Find the value of *y* in the triangle below.

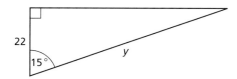

Answer:

_____

_____

Perimeter, Area and Estimation

QUESTION 1   1 mark

Calculate the perimeter (*P*) and area (*A*) of the rectangle shown.

Given the dimensions of the rectangle, estimate the following distances.

- From *d* to *x*.

- From *d* to *y*.

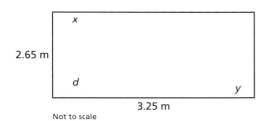

Not to scale

Answer:

_____

_____

_____

_____

QUESTION 2   1 mark

Calculate the perimeter (*P*) and area (*A*) of the rectangle shown.

Given the dimensions of the rectangle, estimate the following distances.

- From *d* to *x*.

- From *d* to *y*.

- From *d* to *z*.

---

d ⌐⌐⌐⌐⌐⌐⌐

z

x   4.55 m

y

3.65 m

Not to scale

Answer:

_____

_____

_____

_____

_____

_____

Tables

QUESTION 1   1 mark

Variation of current with time

Time (milliseconds)	0	0.5	1	1.5	2	2.5	3
Current (amperes)	0	24	45	66	81	89	92

Explain what is happening with respect to the change of current over time in the table above.

Answer:

_____

_____

_____

_____

QUESTION 2   1 mark

Explain what happened to the change in current from 2 to 3 milliseconds.

Answer:

_____

Graphs

QUESTION 1   5 marks

Complete the table below using Ohm's law to find the values for resistance (ohms). The current values in the table are measured at 24 V.

Current (A)	1	2	3	4	5	6	7	8	9
Resistance (Ω)									

Plot a graph that represents the data, showing current (amps) on the x-axis and resistance (ohms) on the y-axis.

Answer:

QUESTION 2   5 marks

Complete the table below, using Ohm's law to find the values for resistance (ohms). The current values in the table are measured at 24 V.

Current (A)	0.4	1.8	2.5	3.7	4.9	7.0	8.3	9.7	10.3	11.9	13.1
Resistance (Ω)											

Plot a graph that represents the data, showing current (amps) on the x-axis and resistance (ohms) on the y-axis.

Answer:

9780170474535

Glossary

Alternating current (AC)   An electric current that changes direction at regular intervals, most commonly at a rate of 50 cycles per second.

Ampere (amp)   The scientific unit used to measure electric current.

Circuit   A circuit is made up of a number of electrical components joined to each other by conducting leads. Circuits are generally operated from a switch that turns the power source on and off as required.

Circuit breaker   A safety device that operates like a fuse, preventing excessive current from flowing into a circuit. Circuit breakers are designed to prevent overheating and electrical fires.

Current   The flow of an electric charge through a conducting media. Current is measured in amperes.

Direct current (DC)   An electric current that flows in only one direction through a circuit.

Fuse   A safety device within a circuit that is designed to break if excessive current passes through it. Fuses help prevent electrical fires and prevent damage to appliances or equipment connected to the circuit.

Insulator   A material that has a very high electrical resistance; it does not generally conduct electricity.

Joule (J)   The standard unit for work and energy.

Ohm (Ω)   A unit of electrical resistance.

Ohm's law   Ohm's law states that the resistance of an electrical component can be determined by dividing the voltage for the component by the current flowing through the component.

Potential difference   The difference in electrical potential between one point in a circuit and another; measured in volts.

Power   The rate at which energy is produced or consumed. There are two formulas that can be used for determining the power in an electric circuit: $P = VI$ or $P = R I^2$.

Resistance   The strength with which a material opposes the flow of an electrical current passing through it. Resistance is measured in ohms (Ω).

Resistor   A component used to regulate the flow of a current within a circuit. The strength of a resistor is measured in ohms (Ω).

Series   The current in a series circuit must follow a certain path, passing through one component after another, in order. The current within a series circuit is the same between each component; therefore, the total resistance in a series circuit can be worked out by adding the strength of all of the resistors together.

Terminal   The attachment point of a power supply; may also be referred to as 'the terminals'.

Volt   The standard unit for potential difference or voltage.

Watt   The unit for power.

Formulae and Data

Calculating the number of watts in a circuit

The formula for calculating the number of watts in a circuit is given as:

$W = VA$

where

W = watts

V = volts

A = amps

Voltage drop

Voltage drop across a resistance when a current is flowing can be calculated using the formula:

$V = IR$ (Ohm's law)

where

V = voltage drop   (unit is volts, V)

I = current   (unit is amps, A)

R = resistance   (unit is ohms, Ω)

Electrical power

The formula used for calculating the value of power from a supply is:

$$P = \frac{V^2}{R}$$

where

P = power   (unit is watts, W)

V = voltage drop   (unit is volts, V)

R = resistance   (unit is ohms, Ω)

Impedance

$$Z = \sqrt{R^2 + X^2}$$

where

Z = impedance   (unit is ohms, Ω)

R = resistance   (unit is ohms, Ω)

X = reactance   (unit is ohms, Ω)

Ohm's law

$$I = \frac{V}{R}$$

where

I = current   (unit is amps, A)

V = potential difference   (unit is volts, V)

R = resistance   (unit is ohms, Ω)

Electrical power in a circuit

A formula that can be used to calculate the value of power in an electrical circuit is given as:

$P = I^2R$

where

P = power $\qquad$ (unit is watts, W)

I = current $\qquad$ (unit is amps, A)

R = resistance $\qquad$ (unit is ohms, Ω)

Resistance in a series circuit

$R_{Total} = R_1 + R_2 + R_3 + \ldots$

e.g. Three resistors are in series in a circuit. $R_1 = 5\,\Omega$, $R_2 = 15\,\Omega$ and $R_3 = 50\,\Omega$.

$$R_{Total} = R_1 + R_2 + R_3$$
$$= 5\,\Omega + 15\,\Omega + 50\,\Omega$$
$$= 70\,\Omega \quad \text{(total resistance)}$$

AC circuits (Pythagoras' theorem)

The formula for Pythagoras' theorem is given as:

$A^2 + B^2 = C^2$

Or, it can also be written as:

$C^2 = A^2 + B^2$

When applied in an electrical context, the values are changed, but the structure of the formula remains the same, thus giving:

$Z^2 = R^2 + X^2$

where

Z = impedance $\qquad$ (unit is ohms, Ω)

R = resistance $\qquad$ (unit is ohms, Ω)

X = reactance $\qquad$ (unit is ohms, Ω)

Efficiency

The electrical efficiency of an electrical device can be calculated using the formula:

$$\text{Efficiency} = \frac{\text{power output}}{\text{power input}} \times 100$$

Percentage of error

$$\text{Percentage of error} = \frac{\text{difference}}{\text{calculated value}} \times 100$$

Trigonometry

Opposite is the side opposite to where the angle is given.
Adjacent is the side that is 'next to' the angle that is given.
Hypotenuse is the longest side of the triangle.

Rule 1

$$\sin \theta = \frac{\text{opposite}}{\text{hypotenuse}}$$

Rule 2

$$\cos \theta = \frac{\text{adjacent}}{\text{hypotenuse}}$$

Rule 3

$$\tan \theta = \frac{\text{opposite}}{\text{adjacent}}$$

Perimeter of a rectangle

Perimeter is the length of all sides added together.
Perimeter = length + breadth + length + breadth
Perimeter = $l + b + l + b$

Area of a rectangle

Area = length $\times$ breadth and is given in square units
Area = $l \times b$

9780170474535

Times Tables

1
1 × 1 = 1
2 × 1 = 2
3 × 1 = 3
4 × 1 = 4
5 × 1 = 5
6 × 1 = 6
7 × 1 = 7
8 × 1 = 8
9 × 1 = 9
10 × 1 = 10
11 × 1 = 11
12 × 1 = 12

2
1 × 2 = 2
2 × 2 = 4
3 × 2 = 6
4 × 2 = 8
5 × 2 = 10
6 × 2 = 12
7 × 2 = 14
8 × 2 = 16
9 × 2 = 18
10 × 2 = 20
11 × 2 = 22
12 × 2 = 24

3
1 × 3 = 3
2 × 3 = 6
3 × 3 = 9
4 × 3 = 12
5 × 3 = 15
6 × 3 = 18
7 × 3 = 21
8 × 3 = 24
9 × 3 = 27
10 × 3 = 30
11 × 3 = 33
12 × 3 = 36

4
1 × 4 = 4
2 × 4 = 8
3 × 4 = 12
4 × 4 = 16
5 × 4 = 20
6 × 4 = 24
7 × 4 = 28
8 × 4 = 32
9 × 4 = 36
10 × 4 = 40
11 × 4 = 44
12 × 4 = 48

5
1 × 5 = 5
2 × 5 = 10
3 × 5 = 15
4 × 5 = 20
5 × 5 = 25
6 × 5 = 30
7 × 5 = 35
8 × 5 = 40
9 × 5 = 45
10 × 5 = 50
11 × 5 = 55
12 × 5 = 60

6
1 × 6 = 6
2 × 6 = 12
3 × 6 = 18
4 × 6 = 24
5 × 6 = 30
6 × 6 = 36
7 × 6 = 42
8 × 6 = 48
9 × 6 = 54
10 × 6 = 60
11 × 6 = 66
12 × 6 = 72

7
1 × 7 = 7
2 × 7 = 14
3 × 7 = 21
4 × 7 = 28
5 × 7 = 35
6 × 7 = 42
7 × 7 = 49
8 × 7 = 56
9 × 7 = 63
10 × 7 = 70
11 × 7 = 77
12 × 7 = 84

8
1 × 8 = 8
2 × 8 = 16
3 × 8 = 24
4 × 8 = 32
5 × 8 = 40
6 × 8 = 48
7 × 8 = 56
8 × 8 = 64
9 × 8 = 72
10 × 8 = 80
11 × 8 = 88
12 × 8 = 96

9
1 × 9 = 9
2 × 9 = 18
3 × 9 = 27
4 × 9 = 36
5 × 9 = 45
6 × 9 = 54
7 × 9 = 63
8 × 9 = 72
9 × 9 = 81
10 × 9 = 90
11 × 9 = 99
12 × 9 = 108

10
1 × 10 = 10
2 × 10 = 20
3 × 10 = 30
4 × 10 = 40
5 × 10 = 50
6 × 10 = 60
7 × 10 = 70
8 × 10 = 80
9 × 10 = 90
10 × 10 = 100
11 × 10 = 110
12 × 10 = 120

11
1 × 11 = 11
2 × 11 = 22
3 × 11 = 33
4 × 11 = 44
5 × 11 = 55
6 × 11 = 66
7 × 11 = 77
8 × 11 = 88
9 × 11 = 99
10 × 11 = 110
11 × 11 = 121
12 × 11 = 132

12
1 × 12 = 12
2 × 12 = 24
3 × 12 = 36
4 × 12 = 48
5 × 12 = 60
6 × 12 = 72
7 × 12 = 84
8 × 12 = 96
9 × 12 = 108
10 × 12 = 120
11 × 12 = 132
12 × 12 = 144

Multiplication Grid

	1	2	3	4	5	6	7	8	9	10	11	12
1	1	2	3	4	5	6	7	8	9	10	11	12
2	2	4	6	8	10	12	14	16	18	20	22	24
3	3	6	9	12	15	18	21	24	27	30	33	36
4	4	8	12	16	20	24	28	32	36	40	44	48
5	5	10	15	20	25	30	35	40	45	50	55	60
6	6	12	18	24	30	36	42	48	54	60	66	72
7	7	14	21	28	35	42	49	56	63	70	77	84
8	8	16	24	32	40	48	56	64	72	80	88	96
9	9	18	27	36	45	54	63	72	81	90	99	108
10	10	20	30	40	50	60	70	80	90	100	110	120
11	11	22	33	44	55	66	77	88	99	110	121	132
12	12	24	36	48	60	72	84	96	108	120	132	144

Notes

Notes

Notes

Notes

9780170474535

Notes

Notes

9780170474535